Wishing Powder

MAGGIE PRINCE

Wishing Powder

Illustrated by Val Biro

HODDER AND STOUGHTON
LONDON SYDNEY AUCKLAND TORONTO

British Library Cataloguing in Publication Data

Prince, Maggie
  Wishing powder.—(Brock red)
  Rn: Balint Stephen Biro   I.Title   II.Biro, Val
  823'.914[J]   PZ7

  ISBN 0-340-38038-1

First published 1986
Second impression 1986

Published by Hodder and Stoughton Children's Books,
a division of Hodder and Stoughton Ltd,
Mill Road, Dunton Green, Sevenoaks, Kent TN13 2YJ

Photoset by Rowland Phototypesetting Ltd,
Bury St Edmunds, Suffolk

Printed in Great Britain by T.J. Press (Padstow) Ltd,
Padstow, Cornwall

Chapter 1

James's tooth had fallen out that morning. It was the top right hand front one. The other front one was wobbly too, and as a result James wasn't speaking any too clearly at all that day, and that was how it started.

'James, would you please go over to the shop and get me some washing powder before you go to school?' shouted Mum from the kitchen. 'I'm in a hurry to get the washing into the machine before I go to work, or you won't have any socks for tomorrow. It's a good thing Mr Barnstaple opens early.'

'All right, Mum,' James mumbled,

feeling his other tooth wanting to swing to and fro like a pendulum. He took the money that his mother held out, and went over the road to the village shop. The old shopkeeper had retired recently, and sold the shop to Mr Barnstaple, a young man with a big black beard.

'Yes, sonny?' Mr Barnstaple appeared, glaring, behind the counter as James entered the shop. The shop doorbell clanged. James wished the old shopkeeper were still there. He had

known all their names. Mr Barnstaple just called them all 'dear' or 'sonny'.

'Some washing powder, please,' muttered James through clamped lips, suddenly realising that he didn't know whether Mum wanted Daz or Ariel. Perhaps it wouldn't matter. Mr Barnstaple peered at him, leaning his elbows on the counter and pushing his face close to James's with a suspicious frown.

'We don't get asked for much of *that*,

you know,' he whispered. James was surprised. The rest of the village must be very dirty. 'Er, how much did you want?' Mr Barnstaple was continuing confidentially. 'One pinch? Two?'

'Oh, you know, about this much.' James drew the shape of a box of washing powder in the air with his hands. Mr Barnstaple rocked back on his heels.

'You use . . . a lot of it then?' he enquired faintly.

'Oh yes. Twice a week.'

Mr Barnstaple's eyes bulged.

'Twice a week. Well well. Truly amazing. Most people would be in a state of total collapse.'

'It's my Mum. She does it. She doesn't get tired at all.'

Mr Barnstaple looked positively awestruck and fetched a red and blue patterned box labelled MIRACLE, a

8

brand which James didn't recognise at all. Anyway, since Mr Barnstaple seemed so odd today, he decided to take it and hope for the best.

James walked home with the box under his arm, realising that he would have to hurry now if he wanted to be in time for school.

'I wish I didn't have to go to school today,' he muttered to himself. 'I wish it would snow, or the school would blow up, or something.'

Overhead the sky took on a dull, yellowish-grey tinge, and in the distance came a muffled clap, like thunder.

When James got home, Mum was on the telephone.

'Good grief!' she said. 'Good gracious! What, just now? Just a few minutes ago? Well thank you for letting me know, Mrs Jones. Yes I would have been setting off with James in about fifteen minutes. No, one doesn't know whether there might be more explosions. What a relief that no-one seems to have been there yet.' She turned to James. 'James, that was Mrs Jones, the school caretaker. She says that the school just blew up.' Outside, feathery white flakes started to drift past the window.

Chapter 2

James was glad he didn't have to go to school. He felt too tired anyway. He put the box labelled MIRACLE down on a worktop in the kitchen and pondered the amazing coincidence that the school had blown up just after he wished that it would. What was more, it was now snowing. The flakes came thicker and faster as he watched, and the ground was already covered. Mum strode into the kitchen in her macintosh and crammed a few last socks into the washing machine.

'Oh dear, this is a nuisance. It's a good thing Android is coming in to clean today, or I should have had to take the day off work.' Mum was a reporter on the local paper, and wrote a column called 'Ruth Parker investigates'. She straightened James's school tie. 'I must go down to the school now and see what I can find out. I expect the boilers blew up. Will you be all right? Android should be here in about ten minutes.'

James nodded. 'I'll be fine.'

Android was their cleaner. His real name was Andrew, but Mum had called him Android from the first moment she saw him, although not to his face. Most of the people whom James knew who had cleaners, had sensible ladies in flowered overalls, but not his Mum. She had a punk. When she and James had gone down to the Job Centre and said they were looking for a cleaner, behind them in the queue had been a frightening-looking Mohican with

safety pins through his ears and nose,
and what looked like a stun gun in his
belt.

'I'll do it, missis,' he said, and that
was that. Andrew was theirs.

At that moment he arrived, bringing
his own broom, which looked more like
his twin brother than anything.

'Wotcher, Roof,'' he said. 'I'll sweep
the snow off the step for you.' His voice
was hoarse and he obviously had a cold.

A drip hung on the end of his safety pin.

'Oh poor Andrew,' said Mum in concern. 'Are you all right? Perhaps you shouldn't work today.'

Android assured her that he was all right, and Mum departed, promising to ring them at lunch-time.

In the kitchen, while Android made himself some coffee and put rather a lot of whisky in it, James told him about the school blowing up. Android was impressed.

'I often used to wish my school would blow up, when I was young, but it never happened. Some people have all the luck.'

Rubbing his eyes, James decided to go back to bed for a while. He couldn't understand why he felt so tired. Why, even his eyes were playing tricks on him. He had just looked at the packet of MIRACLE and thought it said wishing powder instead of washing powder. He looked again. It did say wishing powder. 'MIRACLE WISHING POWDER. No harmful consequences'. James focussed his eyes in astonishment and read the small print. 'Over-use may cause exhaustion. Approved by EEC Commission of Chief Magicians. By appointment to HM the Queen, Purveyors of Potions.'

Suddenly, a lot of things became clear.

Chapter 3

By lunch-time Android's cold was much worse and his voice had gone almost completely. James, however, felt much better, despite the fact that his teacher, Miss Grinch, had sent round some work for him to do at home. He stared at Android sympathetically. Poor Android. It was awful not to be able to speak. Perhaps . . . He went into the kitchen and tipped some of the wishing powder into his hand. It was dull green, and sparkled with lights of purple fire. It was beautiful.

'I wish Andrew's cold was better,' he whispered.

The powder glowed and vanished, leaving just a few traces on James's palm. A loud shout came from the living room.

'Hey! I feel better. My voice has come back!' Android rushed into the kitchen.

'Oh Andrew, I'm so glad. You sound much better. I wish Mum could hear you now.' James hid his hand behind his back guiltily. Android shook his head in bewilderment.

'Well it's certainly a funny old day. What with bombs going off and colds going away.' His voice seemed to echo strangely, and it was only then, as his palm tingled and the gritty feel of the remaining wishing powder vanished, that James realised what he had said. He had just made another wish . . .

Mum normally shopped in her lunch hour in Taunton, and the shops were usually crowded. She had come out of Boots and was just going towards Tesco when she first heard the voices in her head. She shook her head in confusion, then realised that other people were also looking around themselves.

'BOMBS going off,' the voice boomed suddenly. There were gasps all around her.

'Bombs!' exclaimed another woman. 'Who said bombs? Is this a bomb scare?'

People looked at each other in alarm. A woman in a nylon macintosh screamed and fainted. People began to hurry out of the shopping centre, some of them starting to run. A pekingese dog on a lead ran round and round its elderly owner in excitement, tying his legs together. The owner hopped a few steps then fell into a nearby dustcart. Mum, like the good reporter she was, whipped out her notebook and began making

notes. At that moment a policeman appeared out of Boots the Chemist where he had been buying a large bottle of Macho Man Aftershave. He stared in astonishment at the fleeing crowd.

'A bomb!'

'It's going to go off!' people shrieked. An old lady helped the pekingese owner out of the dustcart and sat him on her shopping trolley before racing on. In bewilderment the policeman took out his radio and began calling for reinforcements, his eyes flicking from side to side as people hurtled past him. He spotted Mum, who was trying to interview a young woman in a fur coat whose high heels prevented her from moving very fast.

'Where *is* this bomb?' he asked, moving over to her and nearly being mown down by a jet-propelled baby buggy.

Mum shook her head. 'I don't know.

There was some kind of strange loud-speaker announcement.'

'I'd better call in the army, and the bomb disposal experts. The fire brigade too. Maybe some ambulances just in case. You'd better move along, madam.'

Mum stood her ground. 'I'm Ruth Parker of the Morning Messenger. I need to get an on-the-spot story.'

'I'm sorry madam, you can be the Prime Minister herself for all I care. I shall still have to move you along. I'm evacuating the area.'

In the distance sirens sounded, and as Mum left the shopping centre and started to cross the road an army jeep full of men in camouflage gear screeched to a halt by the pavement. Mum rushed to the nearest telephone box to ring the editor and tell her she had tomorrow's front page news.

Chapter 4

At home James had settled down to do his homework. They were studying dinosaurs at school, and he was supposed to be drawing a pterodactyl. After two attempts he screwed up the paper and sank his head into his hands.

'It's no good. I can't draw pterodactyls,' he muttered to himself. 'It would be a lot easier if I could see one, instead of trying to copy from this stupid book.' Suddenly an idea dawned. It was so alarming that at first he abandoned it straight away, but then, he did have to get his pterodactyl drawn somehow. Rigid with fright he crept downstairs.

Android was in the kitchen dabbing green food colouring on to his fringe. James whistled casually and poured himself a drink of blackcurrant. Somehow he had to get Android out of the kitchen. It had stopped snowing outside now and the sun was shining.

'Do you think Mum would like us to pick the last few roses from the garden before the snow spoils them?' he asked innocently. 'The fresh air might stop your cold from coming back.'

'A good idea, me old son.' Android used up the last of the food colouring to draw a wavy line down his left cheek. 'You know, they remind me of *my* old Mum, those roses.'

'Really?' James was amazed to think of Android as having a Mum, and found it rather touching to hear her compared to a rose.

'Yeah. They've got great big hips.'

He went out into the garden, laughing coarsely.

At once James reached down the wishing powder and poured some into his hand.

'I wish I could see a pterodactyl. A *friendly* pterodactyl,' he added hastily. The wishing powder glittered with its purple lights and vanished. James waited.

He was still waiting when Android came back into the kitchen with a bunch of frostbitten roses and began arranging them in a jam jar.

'I reckon next door's cat's got hisself locked in the garden shed again,' he said. 'There's a terrible racket going on in there. I'll let him out when I've put these flowers in water.'

James's eyes widened.

'Oh, I'll do it,' he said hastily, rushing to the back door. He slammed it

24

behind him and ran up the garden, his feet making small footprints in the snow next to Android's huge Dr Marten's ones.

The walls of the small wooden garden shed were shaking, and something was visible moving to and fro at the dark dusty window. James stopped, afraid to open the door. He had specified a *friendly* pterodactyl, and the packet had said that the wishing powder had no harmful consequences. All the same, whatever was in there sounded as though it had the size and personality of a rhinoceros. At last he found enough courage to lift the latch and open the door a crack. At once he was knocked flat on his back, and a huge leathery wing flapped wildly in the open doorway. In panic James leapt to his feet and crammed the wing back inside the shed. A greenish narrow face with a long sharp beak peered at him from near the ceiling, and suddenly the creature became still.

'Aaark,' it said.

'Oh,' said James. 'Oh, aren't you amazing.'

The creature folded its wings, immediately seeming much smaller, and sidled towards him. Its horny feet made

a dry clack clacking on the wooden floor. It tripped over a bicycle and fell beak first into a box of daffodil bulbs. James reached over and helped it steady itself.

'Aaark,' it said, and came and put its head on his shoulder.

'Oh.' James was quite overcome. 'Can you just wait a moment and I'll get my drawing pad?' He patted the pterodactyl on its head. Its skin felt dry and rough, like carpet. Smiling at it reassuringly, he edged his way out of the shed. At once the pterodactyl went mad again. James rushed back in.

'Shhh,' he cooed soothingly. 'It's all right. I'll be back in a minute.' The pterodactyl looked very upset and went round the shed in a lot of little jumps with its feet together. At that moment James heard Android coming up the garden.

'Oh dear.' He peered frantically through the small window. Android had his broom and was obviously going to sweep the garden path clear of snow. He was coming towards the shed. James poked his head out and beamed nonchalantly.

'Hello, Andrew,' he murmured. But the pterodactyl obviously thought he was leaving again.

'Aaark!' it screeched, and began to bat its giant wings against the flimsy wooden walls.

'Gordon Bennett, what's that?' exclaimed Android. James reached one arm back in and grabbed the pterodactyl by the neck.

'Oh, n-nothing. Er, that is, it's just a friend, a er ptero, um Terry, that's who it is. My friend Terry.'

'Well he ain't half noisy. You mind he don't do no damage in there.'

'I will. Oh, er, Andrew, I don't suppose you'd bring my drawing pad up here would you? I thought I'd do a bit a drawing with Terry.'

'Good idea. At least it'll be a bit quieter.' Android went back down the garden to get the drawing pad.

Chapter 5

The pterodactyl sat very still while James drew him, and James knew it was one of the best drawings he had ever done. It was starting to become dark outside by the time he had finished. As he put the last touches to it he heard his mother's voice from the bottom of the garden.

'Where's James, Andrew?'

'Up the garden in the shed, Roof, playing with his friend Terry.'

Mum's voice came nearer. 'Terry? I don't remember any Terry. He must be new round here.'

'Shhh. Keep still.' James clamped his

hand round the pterodactyl's beak and leaned out of the shed.

'Hello, Mum. Had a good day?'

'Well yes, rather an eventful one. Who's this Terry? What's his other name?'

'Oh, er, Dactyl. He's new round here. He only arrived today.'

'Oh. That's an unusual name. Is he foreign?'

'Um, actually Mum we're playing a secret game. Don't come into the shed. It'll spoil it. I'll come into the house in a minute.'

'Oh well all right. I'm going to make tea so don't be long.' She went back down the garden, and James knew she would be glad to have a few minutes on her own to put her feet up and have a cup of tea. In the meantime he had to find a way of keeping the pterodactyl quiet while he went to get the wishing

powder to make it vanish again. The
creature was becoming very affectionate
and kept ruffling James's hair with its
beak.

'I'll be quite sorry to see you go,' he
said to it sadly.

After several attempts to leave with-
out upsetting it, James finally realised
that he was just going to have to shut it
in, and hope that no-one heard the
noise. With any luck on a cold autumn
tea-time everyone would be drawing
their curtains and settling down in front
of their television sets. With a swift leap
he escaped from the shed and slammed
the door behind him.

James thought the garden shed would
disintegrate behind him as he hurried
down the path and into the kitchen. It
was warm and welcoming indoors and
the kitchen smelled of baking. James
saw that Android had been making

some of his multi-coloured punk cakes. He hurriedly jammed a couple into his trouser pockets. The pterodactyl was sure to be hungry, and he could hardly send it back to its prehistoric age on an empty stomach. Then he looked around for the wishing powder. It was not where he had left it. Next to him the washing machine hummed and rotated, full of clothes and water. An appalling

suspicion struck James. At that moment Android called from the hall.

'Cheerio James. Cheerio Roof. I put the rest of the washing in for you. That wasn't half funny washing powder you've got. All glittery like. See you on Friday then.' The front door banged and he was gone.

James thought he might faint. The wishing powder was all gone. Android had tipped it into the washing machine and he was lumbered with a pterodactyl and no wishing powder. What was worse, Mr Barnstaple's shop would now be shut for the night. Outside, the thumping and drumming from the top of the garden became louder. Perhaps he could find the empty box. There might be just enough left in it for one more wish. He rummaged in the bin, becoming smeared with tealeaves and some of yesterday's leftover spinach. It wasn't there. In desperation he ran into the living room where Mum was sprawled on the sofa watching the news and drinking a mug of steaming tea. The fire which Android had made earlier burnt up warmly, and in it a singed piece of red cardboard with the letters MIRAC on it, flared up and turned to ash.

Hunched, James left the room. Whatever was he to do? He took one of the punk cakes for himself and trailed up the garden, eating it. The pterodactyl greeted him rapturously, rubbing its head up and down his neck and curling its wings behind its back. James fed it the punk cakes.

'Aaark.' The fierce-looking, beaky mouth gobbled them down and it looked hopefully for more.

'Still hungry? All right, I'll get you something else.' He stepped to open the door, but it was dark now and he stumbled. The door swung open and James was bowled over amid clanging bicycle bells as the pterodactyl rushed past him and out into the night.

'Hey! Come back! Ptero . . . er, Terry . . .' He grinned foolishly as his mother appeared out of the gloom.

'Hasn't your friend gone home yet, James? It's getting rather late.'

'He's gone now, Mum.' He slid his eyes sideways to where a large, dark shape had just taken off from the top of the fence. The draught from the downbeat of its wings buffeted them.

'Goodness, that wind's getting up. Come on in now. It's time for tea.'

With James looking nervously over his shoulder, they went into the house.

Chapter 6

It must have been around midnight when James woke and realised what he had to do. He lay very still in bed and thought through the plan which had come to him in his sleep. Burglary. It was the only answer. He must break into Mr Barnstaple's shop and steal some more wishing powder. It wasn't normally the sort of thing he would have done, but this was a desperate situation. After all, if shops were silly enough to close when people most needed them, then they must expect to be burgled, he decided. He listened carefully, then climbed out of bed.

James's bed was the sort which is up a wooden ladder and has a wardrobe and built-in desk below. Android had made it when he first came to them. The ladder creaked now as James reached the floor. He stopped and listened again, but there was only the sound of Mum safely snoring next door. He opened his wardrobe door and took out a pair of warm trousers and a thick black sweater, and changed into them. The wardrobe door squeaked on its hinges as he closed it. His old trainers had their laces in knots so he decided to stay in his furry bedroom slippers. Silently he crept downstairs, the banister and win-dowseat unfamiliar in the darkness. He peered briefly out through the landing window at the night. The village looked empty and mysterious. Stars shone, and the patches of snow which remained, reflected their light. Pausing only to put on his anorak in the hall, James tiptoed out into the cold, midnight, village street.

It only took him two minutes to reach Mr Barnstaple's shop. One dim light shone inside, over the post office counter. The door was securely locked. He could see the padlocks and chains through the glass from the outside. High on the wall a burglar alarm glinted in the starlight, topped with a swirl of snow like a piece of gateau. How was he to get in?

Just then he saw Mr Barnstaple's cat, Pluto. It was black and fluffy, and it padded right past him on noiseless feet to the side of the house. James followed it, and watched it leap on to a small windowsill, then wriggle in through an open window. Sick with hope, James hauled himself on to the windowsill too, tilted his head, and peered in.

He couldn't believe his luck. It was the store room. Tins of food, boxes of soap powder and detergent, cartons of butter and sweets and toilet rolls, and all the things which Mr Barnstaple sold in his shop, were stacked around the walls. A small table heaped with papers stood at the far side, and the cat had gone and curled up in a basket underneath it. On a shelf above the table were five red and blue boxes labelled MIRACLE.

Cautiously James felt around the small open window for a catch to open it further, then realised despairingly that it was nailed into position. Inside and outside it was fastened with six inch nails. With a groan James slithered back to the ground. It was no good. He would have to break in some other way. If he left the pterodactyl until morning then everyone would see it, and it would get into all the papers, and he would never

live it down at school. With Mum
around, everything got into the papers.

He felt in his pocket for his penknife.
He would have to try and force the
latch. If the alarm sounded perhaps he

could get away before anyone caught him. Instead of a penknife his fingers came into contact with something sticky. It was disgusting, wet and slimy. Pieces attached themselves to his fingers. He withdrew his hand quickly and realised that it was half a packet of chocolate buttons, left over from last week's sweets. It had ripped down one side, and the gooey mess had melted against his warm leg. He licked his finger. It still tasted good. Suddenly an idea occurred to him. If *he* liked the chocolate, then maybe the *cat* would too. He grinned at it nervously, then eased the torn packet of chocolate buttons out of his pocket and climbed back on to the windowsill.

'Pluto,' he called. The cat lay unmoving under the table and opened one eye.

'Pluto! Here! Come and taste this.'

James tossed one clammy chocolate

drop through the window. It fell with a splat on to the linoed floor. The cat uncoiled itself and stared at it suspiciously. James threw another one, harder this time. It hit the cat on the nose. With a swipe the cat flattened the chocolate drop to the floor, then lifted a chocolatey paw and licked it. It licked it again, then stuffed its paw into its mouth and sucked it. That drop gone, it didn't take the cat long to find the other one underneath the window, and to eat that too. Then it stared at James hopefully, its eyes like headlamps in its black fur. It really did look like a magician's cat. Trying to appear casual, it patrolled to and fro several times beneath the window, then jumped up on to the windowsill. James threw a couple more chocolate drops in to keep it happy. The cat slurped them up and looked expectantly for more. Carefully James angled

his whole arm through the window. It was a tight fit and he crunched his funnybone on the big iron latch. The cat jumped up and down hysterically.

'All right, Pluto. Here's another one. Go and get it.' James flung another chocolate drop as hard as he could towards the shelf of wishing powder. It landed first time, smearing itself messily down the side of one of the packets, and sliding to a halt on the dusty shelf.

44

The cat leapt half a metre into the air
and raced round and round the small
room.

'*There*, you idiot,' James shouted.
'On the shelf!'

The cat mewed pathetically and
swarmed up the window and into
James's arms.

Chapter 7

James almost sobbed in desperation as the cat slobbered over his chocolatey hand. '*No*! Go and get *that* one, stupid.' He eased the cat's bulky form back through the window and pointed it towards the shelf of wishing powder. It yelped and scrambled back up his arm.

James drew a deep breath.

'Right cat, now let's be reasonable about this.' He tucked the cat firmly under one arm, where it squirmed playfully and tried to bite his ear. It seemed to weight at least twenty kilos. With his other hand James separated a couple more chocolate drops, and fed one to the cat. It drooled blissfully and gave a satisfied burp.

'Oh no, you can't be full yet.' James held the other chocolate drop under the cat's nose, then put his arm through the open window again and tossed the sticky brown mess across the room. The cat took off like a guided missile, knocking down tins and boxes and crashing into cartons. It hit the table at about seventy miles an hour, and hurtled up one leg. Packets of wishing powder rained down on its head, and with a whumph one burst open. Glittering green dust lit up the night and the cat was covered in it, like a picture in neon lights. Triumphantly it gobbled down the chocolate drop. James sighed with relief and stretched his aching knees. Now came the hard part. He counted the chocolate drops which remained. There were three left.

The cat seemed strangely tired after its record-breaking sprint. It slid down a leg of the table and landed with a thud like a bean bag.

'Pluto,' James called softly. 'Pluto, come and have some more chocolate.'

The cat gazed at James and its eyes started to close.

'Oh no.' James wiped a chocolatey hand across his forehead. 'Just one more, Pluto. *Please.*' He held out the three remaining chocolate drops, which by now had almost become one large one. Perhaps if he pretended to be a mouse. 'Eeeek eeeek,' his whispered. The fluorescent cat cocked one ear and regarded him disbelievingly.

'Here Pluto, here.' The chocolate had formed ridges along the lines of James's hand. Slowly the cat stood up and stretched, then padded slowly towards him. James dangled his arm temptingly

through the window, swinging it from
the elbow. Grudgingly the cat jumped
on to the windowsill, and as it did so,
James grabbed it. Almost dislocating
his shoulder he hauled it through the
window and hugged it.

'Blerk!' The cat hiccupped like an exploding pillow and the wishing powder blasted out all over James. He coughed and spluttered, then fed the cat the last of the chocolate drops, which now resembled nothing that Cadbury's would ever have recognised. He looked down at himself. He glowed. If anyone saw him returning through the village they would think they were seeing a ghost.

'Thanks, cat,' he muttered, then tipped it back through the window and headed for home.

Chapter 8

James was very tired when he got home, but he concentrated hard and tiptoed upstairs silently. In his room, he stood and thought out his wish carefully. He must make no mistakes. He only had one wish, as the wishing powder was stuck to him and it wouldn't be possible to save any for later. The house was very quiet. Even Mum had stopped snoring next door now.

'I wish,' said James slowly, 'that the pterodactyl which appeared in my garden shed would go safely back to its own time, immediately.'

The powder glowed and vanished.

James sagged with exhaustion, and stil
in his clothes, stretched out his hands to
grasp his ladder and climb into bed. A
that moment Mum walked in.

'James! I thought I heard something
. . .' Her voice trailed away as she saw
his outstretched hands. In the dimness
James crossed his eyes and let his mouth
loll open, then started to walk stiff-
legged across the room. 'James . . .'

Hastily Mum placed herself between him and the window. 'James,' she said in soothing tones, 'you're sleepwalking, darling. Now come and let's get you back into bed.' She peered at him and gave a little yelp as she saw his face. 'Oh dear James, you must have been having nightmares.' She steered him back towards the bed. James gave a loud snore followed by a tonsil-flapping whistle. By now he genuinely *was* having trouble keeping his eyes open. That wish had taken all his strength, and his knees felt ready to buckle. Climbing the ladder stiff-legged and cross-eyed almost finished him off.

At the top he keeled over on to the bed, and the last thing he remembered was Mum stroking his forehead and saying, 'Sleep tight, James.'

The first thing he knew next morning

was the telephone ringing. James strug
gled awake and realised that he was stil
in his trousers and sweater. He could
hear Mum's voice in the hall.

'. . . a sighting? What, near here?
Yes, I'll certainly investigate . . .'

James got up. It was nice not to have
to get dressed. He went downstairs
straightening his clothes and yawning
and found Mum putting her welling
tons on by the front door.

'James, ah, you're up.' She peered a
him anxiously. 'Do you know that you
were sleepwalking last night? You'd
even got dressed.' James was silent, bu
Mum went on. 'Now James, that was
my editor on the phone. There's been a
sighting of some strange giant animal in
a tree over near Blackditch. It's causing
quite a commotion and the editor wants
me to get a report. I'm just going to ring
Android and ask him to come on over

for an hour. All right?'

James went pale and stared at her, then nodded speechlessly. Mum patted his head whilst dialling with her other hand.

'Good boy. I don't expect I'll be long. It's *supposed* to be my morning off.'

James hurried to the back door and looked out. It *couldn't* be the pterodactyl. Could it? Was there some reason why the wishing powder might not have worked? As James poured cornflakes into his breakfast bowl he realised that he would have to do some investigating of his own.

Chapter 9

It was the fastest breakfast he had ever eaten, with milk dripping off his chin and almost as many cornflakes on the outside of his stomach as on the inside.

Android, who only had to cycle over from the neighbouring village, arrived as he was finishing.

'Beast of Blackditch,' muttered Mum, scribbling in her notebook. 'Right you two, see you later.' She hurried out and jumped into her car.

As soon as the exhaust fumes had vanished round the corner, James went to look for Android. His hair was pink today, and he was shivering in the back garden, in his underpants, while he ran the lawnmower over his jeans to make them look more ragged.

'Andrew, please can I go to the shop to buy some crisps?'

Android looked round at him and adjusted his graffiti spray-gun in its shoulder holster.

'Ain't yer Mum got some? She's normally got some in the kitchen cupboard.'

'Oh, but I want a special flavour,' James said firmly.

'What flavour's that then?' Android was really being difficult today.

'Pterodactyl flavour . . . er, that is, er . . . jellied yak toes flavour.'

Android's eyebrows almost disappeared into his pink fringe.

'Cor. Go on then. I don't suppose there's any danger from that big animal yer Mum told me about.'

James hurried off to the shop. His trousers were all crumpled from sleeping in them, his loose tooth felt awkward and uncomfortable, and he could have done with another ten hours' sleep. Things were really getting a bit out of hand, but he must keep a grip on himself and find out if the pterodactyl really was still around. He had a pound coin from his money box, and if necessary he would have to spend it on another whole box of wishing powder.

At the top of the lane he passed Mr Barnstaple's cat, Pluto, again. It was hiding in a wide drain outlet, moving its eyes to and fro nervously. At the shop itself the side window was still jammed open. Suddenly James paused. Something glittered on the ground. Cautiously he sneaked along the side wall of the shop to have a closer look, then groaned. It was wishing powder. The blast from the cat must have covered the ground as well as himself. Worse still, however, were the footprints. There were his, the cat's, and some others. The others were what worried him. They were huge, birdlike clawprints. They were depressingly familiar.

At that moment James heard a police

siren in the distance. He scuttled guiltily round to the front of the shop and stood with his collar up, looking at the display in the window. Seconds later a police car roared into view and stopped by the shop. James edged away. Two uniformed policemen, a tall fat one and a short thin one, got out.

'Right sir,' said the tall fat one as Mr Barnstaple came hurrying out of the shop with the doorbell clanging, 'a break-in you say? Better let us have all the details.'

James fled back towards home.

Chapter 10

It was obvious what had happened. He had wished the pterodactyl away, and it, with wishing powder on its feet, had wished itself straight back again. It was probably looking for him. Oh dear, why had he specified a *friendly* pterodactyl? Perhaps this one had become so fond of him and its new environment that it would never go back to its previous time. James passed the cat again and stroked it. Pluto purred and licked his hand as though hoping for more chocolate drops. It was probably having a nervous breakdown if it had encountered the pterodactyl, James thought.

Unexpectedly some glittering green dust fell out of the cat's right ear and into James's hand. James gaped.

'Wishing powder!' he whispered. 'Oh Pluto, this might solve everything.' Clutching the wishing powder in his hand he ran the rest of the way to his house.

Mum had arrived back home before him, and was talking to Android.

'Nothing!' she was saying in disgust. 'Not a sausage. I think the villagers must have made up the whole story to get publicity for their village fête. They said, would you believe it, that a pterodactyl was sitting up a tree in the old rookery this morning, and flew off in this direction just after nine. I ask you . . .'

At that moment there was a noise in the chimney.

James's house, although small, was

very old, and had a very wide hearth and broad old-fashioned chimney. If you stood in the fireplace when the fire was out you could see right up to a tiny spot of sky far above.

Quietly, James left Mum going on about wasting her time, and tiptoed into the living room. The noise came again. It was a dry rasping against the bricks. He climbed over the brass fender and pushed the previous night's burnt logs to one side with his foot. Then he peered upwards. There was no spot of light. Instead, a dollop of soot hit him in the eye.

'Aaark,' said a pleased voice far above his head. 'Aaark, aaark.'

At that moment the police arrived. James saw them coming up the garden path, then a thunderous knocking shook the front door. Everyone in the house jumped.

'Good gracious! Who can that be?'
exclaimed Mum.

'Sounds like James's friend, Terry,'
said Android.

James wiped the soot from his eye
and crept to the living room door.

'Good morning, madam.' It was the
tall fat policeman. 'I am Sergeant Mangold and this is Constable Cleaver.
We're just making a few routine en-
quiries about a break-in at the shop.'

Mum's eyes widened and she whipped out her notebook again.

'A break-in! Oh wonderful. Would
you like to tell me all about it? I repre-
sent the Morning Messenger. How
much was taken?'

The sergeant looked startled.

'Well nothing much was *taken*,
madam, just a spot of vandalism really.
Washing powder thrown about, that
sort of thing. But we *do* have a clue of

sorts, and that is a trail of chocolate and an empty chocolate drops packet.'

James groaned and closed his eyes. Mum had told him never to drop litter, and now he knew why.

Mum was scribbling in her notebook. She had torn out the sheet which said 'Beast of Blackditch', and was now writing 'Chocolate drop intruder strikes at Chitterford'. As she did so the two policemen began staring suspiciously at Android in his shredded jeans and studded belt. The sergeant seemed about to speak when there was a loud crash in the living room. All four adults ran in, tripping over James, and Pluto the cat, which had slunk in through the open front door. They all gasped. A large rock had fallen into the hearth. It was about the size of a television set, and was the sort of golden-brown hamstone of which the chimney was made.

'Looks like your chimney's coming down, madam,' commented the small thin constable.

'Listen!' Mum frowned. 'There's something up there. I can hear it!'

Android was stroking Pluto the cat. Glittering dust soon covered his hand. 'I wish them two was up there,' he whispered jokingly to James.

There was a whoosh. A gust of air surged round the room, and with a suction noise like a vacuum cleaner, the two policemen shot up the chimney.

'Oh!'

'Blimey!'

Mum and Android were speechless.

'That must have been a whirlwind,' stuttered Android at last. He rushed over to the hearth and looked up the chimney. Echoing down the dark cavernous space came two small plaintive voices.

'Help!'

'Help! Get us down!'

Outside, a large shadow briefly darkened the window and was gone.

The cat, petrified and miaowing, was rubbing itself against Mum's legs. Tiny, sparkling fragments of wishing powder attached themselves to her trousers.

'Oh dear,' croaked Mum. 'We'll have to get them down. How awful. I can't understand how that happened. It was like a tornado, wasn't it? I've never seen anything like it. I haven't got a long ladder to get them down with, either. They sound terrified. I wish there were some way we could just get straight up there and help them.'

The sound was like a hurricane, and James felt himself being lifted from his feet. He tried to grab on to the furniture, but it was no good. The chimney hurtled towards him, a yawning black mouth, then he was inside it and flying upwards, his arms and legs thumping against the sides. Soot and dust choked him, then fresh air blew around his head and with a thud he spun out of the top and landed on the roof. Mum was there already, black with soot, and Android followed straight after, coming down on his graffiti gun, which released a large spurt of green paint into the face of the tall fat sergeant.

'Cor,' said Android, looking round him, 'what a view!'

'Caw,' said a passing crow.

James looked around at the sunlit landscape which stretched far below them. The village of tiny toy houses wound down to the river. The fields and hills behind them, scattered with drifts of fallen autumn leaves, changed colour as clouds passed overhead. The snow had gone now, and something else had gone too. The pterodactyl was nowhere to be seen.

Guiltily Mum, James and Android looked at the two policemen, Constable Cleaver who still pivoted gently on the point of the roof, and was obviously in an advanced state of shock, and Sergeant Mangold who was standing up slowly and ominously, wiping green paint from his cheeks with a sooty hand.

'Madam,' said the sergeant very quietly, 'I am placing you all under arrest.'

Chapter 11

It was half an hour before a neighbour saw the group of them on the roof of James's house and went to borrow a ladder to get them down. Mum spent the entire time apologising to the policemen, while James and Android sat glumly on the ridge of the roof wondering how long they would spend in prison.

When at last their neighbour, a tall, thin, shortsighted woman called Mrs Gurning, appeared staring anxiously at them over the rim of the gutter, they were very pleased indeed to see her.

'My word, officer,' Mrs Gurning

exclaimed, wrinkling up her eyes at the green and black smeared sergeant, 'I do believe you're going mouldy up here in the damp. Now follow me carefully down, all of you.' She took hold of the gutter and prepared to step off into thin air. James grabbed her by the arm just in time.

'No no, Mrs Gurning. The ladder's here.'

They all had to help Constable Cleaver on to the ladder. His rigid limbs and glassy stare made him look like a robot, and he still seemed incapable of speech.

'See what you've done?' snarled Sergeant Mangold as he smacked the constable briskly over the head to get him moving down the ladder.

To their relief, by the time they reached the police car however, Constable Cleaver seemed to be returning to

72

normal, apart from occasional little whimpers and a bad twitch in his right eye.

They set off, with James, Android and Mum in the back. Sergeant Mangold switched the siren on and James shrank his head into his shoulders hoping that no-one he knew would see him. At the police station Sergeant Mangold did a handbrake turn into the nearest parking space and leapt out with a flourish.

'Don't try to get away,' he snapped at Android who was helping Mum out of the car. 'There's no way you're going to get out of *this*.'

James began to feel very alarmed. Were they all about to be locked up? On the police station steps people stared at them and giggled. James tried to wipe the soot from his face, but only succeeded in smearing it even further.

Inside the police station the constable behind the counter looked at them and sniggered.

'I say, sarge, what fantastic makeup. Maybe you've overdone the eyeshadow just a tiny bit though.'

Sergeant Mangold glared at him and the constable's smile faded. 'Er, sorry sarge.'

The sergeant grasped Mum and Android firmly by their arms. 'These persons, constable, are all under arrest. Kindly book them.'

The constable narrowed his eyes and took up his pen in a businesslike manner.

'Right. What's the charge, sarge? Assaulting a police officer? Grievous bodily harm? Resisting arrest? Obstructing an officer in the course of his duty?'

'Yes. The lot. Then you'd better call

the police psychologist to have a look at Constable Cleaver.'

Mum held out her hand to take hold of James's, protectively. It was then that he realised his fist was still full of something. Cautiously he unclenched it a little and sneaked a look. Of course! He still had the wishing powder from the cat's right ear.

'This is ridiculous!' Mum was saying crossly. 'You can't possibly blame us for freak weather conditions. There's no way we could be held responsible for a whirlwind which sucked you up the chimney. Now let us go this minute. I'll pay to have your uniform cleaned, sergeant . . . Don't interrupt, James. This nonsense has gone *quite* far enough . . . 'James! Don't interrupt!'

But James's voice rang out, loud and clear.

'I WISH . . .' he bellowed, 'THAT

YOU WOULD JUST LET US OFF AND THAT WE COULD GO HOME.'

In James's hand the wishing powder fizzed and tickled. In the police station Sergeant Mangold shook himself sharply. Constable Cleaver rubbed his eyes and stretched.

'We-e-ll.' The sergeant looked bemused. 'Well maybe I am being a *little* bit hard on you all.'

'Yes.' Constable Cleaver and the desk officer nodded vigorously. Mum fell silent in astonishment.

'I daresay you couldn't help what happened to us,' the sergeant went on. 'After all, you all ended up on the roof too, didn't you, and I expect you're feeling a bit shaken yourselves. How about a nice cup of tea? Maybe you'd like to clean yourselves up a bit too, then Constable Cleaver can take you home in the car. Take a seat. Get them some cushions, constable. I'll put the kettle on.' He bustled away, and Mum and Android collapsed on to the wooden bench by the door and gaped at each other in amazement.

'Blimey Roof, you didn't half tell 'em!' Android exclaimed admiringly. Mum nodded and straightened her back.

'It was nothing, Andrew. Just calmness and common sense, that's all it takes. You speak sensibly to them and they'll speak sensibly to you.' She turned to James. 'Come and sit down, James, and next time don't interrupt me when I'm speaking to people.'

James wiped his hand on his trousers and went and sat next to his mother.

Chapter 12

It was nearly teatime when they arrived back home.

'We'll never live this down,' muttered Mum as the police car speeded down the lane and their neighbours' curtains twitched.

Indoors, Android put the kettle on and made them another pot of tea, but no sooner had they started drinking it than a large green van with a sun on the side pulled up outside the cottage.

'Oh no.' Mum paused with the cup half way to her lips. James and Android looked at the van and then questioningly at Mum.

'It's the television people,' she groaned. 'The local news must want to know about our freak weather conditions.'

James's mouth dropped open. He might appear on television. He and Android exchanged delighted glances and they both rushed to open the door.

'Oh no! Don't let them in!' Mum shouted, but it was too late. As soon as the door was open, three men with lights and cameras marched in, followed by two women with sheafs of paper and microphones.

'Mrs Parker!' cried the second woman, as though greeting a long-lost friend. 'I'm Melanie Brickbat of Sunset Television News, and I'd like to do a short piece on the whirlwind which hit your house earlier today. This is my sound recordist and these are my lighting experts and cameraman.'

The sound recordist shot her arm up Mum's cardigan and fastened a small microphone on a long wire to her neck.

'Now Mrs Parker, would you like to tell us in your own words what happened?'

James and Android pushed their faces close to the camera and smiled their widest smiles. James wished his teeth didn't look so gappy.

'I'm sorry,' said Mum in a steely

voice, 'but this story is an exclusive of the Morning Messenger.' She clamped her lips firmly together. The television crew stared at each other in dismay and the cameraman stepped backwards on to Pluto the cat who had just come back into the house behind them.

'Oh Mrs Parker, be reasonable. Our viewers would be so interested.'

'Well, perhaps if I were to telephone my editor we could come to some arrangement . . .'

'Yes, yes.' Melanie Brickbat swept up the receiver and thrust it at Mum. 'Telephone your editor. Do. Let's see what she says.'

Grudgingly Mum began to dial, and as she was doing so, James was thinking. If he was to appear on television he really ought to look his best, and this loose tooth and gummy smile were such a sight. He crept past the lighting expert who was fixing a spotlight on to the coat-stand in the hall, and picked up Pluto the cat. With the heavy, purring animal under his arm, he tiptoed away into the kitchen and closed the door.

'Now Pluto,' he whispered, putting the cat down in the vegetable rack, 'let's see if there's any of that wishing powder left inside your *other* ear.' He turned the cat's head and shook it. The cat purred more loudly, thinking that this was a good game, and out of its left ear cascaded a waterfall of glittering dust. Delightedly James caught it in his hand.

'I wish . . .' he said quickly, 'I wish that all this business of loose teeth was over, and that I had all my permanent teeth.'

It was like being electrocuted. A great surge of power shot through his mouth and suddenly it felt very full and cramped. His lips stuck out. He could almost see them by squinting downwards past his nose. The teeth themselves felt as though they stretched right back to his ears. He must have grown *all* his permanent teeth, including his wisdom teeth. He'd better go and have a look.

He crept out of the kitchen and into the dining room next door where a mirror hung on the wall. Apprehensively he gave a small, cautious grin, and nearly

collapsed. The teeth bulged out of his mouth as though they were going to take a bite out of the mirror. He could barely close his lips again over them. He must have grown all his adult teeth in their *adult size*.

James went to the dining room door and listened. Mum and the television crew were still arguing in the hall. He went back to the mirror and prised up one corner of his mouth, then decided he would have to be brave, and gave himself an enormous grin.

It was terrifying. It was like meeting an orang-utan. He backed away from the mirror. The piano was next to him, and as he glanced at it James realised that he bore a striking resemblance to it.

'James! James!' His mother's voice called loudly from the hall. 'Come and be in the picture, dear.'

Oh no. Mum had obviously changed her mind and agreed to give an interview, but he couldn't go in there looking like this. He pulled his lips shut with his fingers as Android burst into the room.

'Come on, me old fruit! We're going to be on the box!' He grabbed James by the wrist, and dragged him into the hall.

Chapter 13

The television crew and Mum had moved into the living room now, and were setting up their equipment round the hearth.

'Sorry Roof, I ain't had time to lay the fire yet,' apologised Android as they all stood by last night's dead logs. But Mum was staring at James who had accidentally giggled when the sound recordist fastened a microphone to his shirt collar.

'*James*, what *have* you got in your mouth?' she hissed in his ear.

James's grin vanished and he felt himself going red.

'Teeth, Mum. Sort of magic, trick teeth.'

'Out of your joke box? Put them away immediately.'

James sucked his lips closed and pretended he hadn't heard. He was saved from further reply by Melanie Brickbat who started positioning them around the room and telling them not to be nervous.

'This is a much bigger story than I'd anticipated,' she beamed. 'I'm going to make quite a large feature of it. Terribly unusual to have a tornado in Somerset.'

The spotlighting came on and the camera whirred. Mum described how first the policemen and then they themselves had been sucked up the chimney that morning. James was asked if he had been scared, and he replied truthfully and in a muffled voice that he had, a bit. Android suggested that a similar freak wind might have caused the havoc in Mr Barnstaple's store room. Everyone seemed to think that this was very likely.

At last the television crew packed all their equipment back into their green van and got ready to go.

'What beautiful teeth he has, for a child,' Melanie Brickbat remarked to Mum as she shook James by the hand. Mum smiled weakly and said goodbye, but James was already halfway into the kitchen.

'Pluto!' he whispered urgently. 'Pluto, where are you?' He grabbed the cat from where it had gone to sleep among the potatoes in the vegetable rack, and shook it violently. There *must* be some wishing powder left on it.

'Blimey! What are you doing to that poor animal?' exclaimed Android as he came through the kitchen door. James put the cat down miserably. There was not a grain of wishing powder left.

'Nothing,' he mumbled, and went out through the back door. All he wanted now were his own loose, wobbly, unreliable teeth back. It was after half past five, but he wandered up in the direction of the shop anyway. Then, as he rounded the corner of the lane, a sudden thought struck him. The footprints outside the store room window! There was wishing powder there, on the ground. He began to run. What if it had been swept up, or blown away by the wind? But no, there it was, dusty and mixed with gravel, but glittering still. The only trouble was that two people were standing in the middle of it. One of them was Mrs Gladstone the postwoman, and the other was Miss Grinch, his teacher.

James sauntered past the front of the

shop and read the notices in the window. He hummed and pretended to check the times of postal collections. He scraped a dirty mark off his anorak. The two women went on talking. They seemed very engrossed in what they were saying. Would they actually notice if he crept round and removed some of the gravel from around their feet? James got down on his hands and knees and started to crawl furtively round the corner of the shop.

'. . . so I said to him, I said "That's the last time I tell you" . . .' Mrs Gladstone talked and Miss Grinch nodded and listened. James found it excruciatingly painful crawling on his hands and knees on gravel, but he was nearly at the wishing powder now and they hadn't seen him yet.

Suddenly Mrs Gladstone gave a shriek.

'Eeeek! Oh, I thought it was a dog. I can't stand dogs. James Parker, whatever are you doing down there?'

'Oh . . .' James looked from one to the other of them. Miss Grinch seemed to be on the verge of laughing. 'I . . . er . . .' He felt his teeth wanting to burst out between his lips in a big snarl.

'Well James?' Miss Grinch smiled at him.

'Miss . . .' He sighed. Oh well. 'Miss, you'll never believe this, but you see I need some of this gravel to get rid of a pterodactyl and a large set of teeth, so if you don't mind I'll just scrape a bit from round your feet. Sorry to disturb you.'

Miss Grinch laughed. 'Oh it's a *game*. I *see*.' She turned to Mrs Gladstone. 'I gave them a project to do on dinosaurs. It's lovely to see how it grips their imagination.'

The two women chuckled merrily and James filled his pockets with gravel and wishing powder.

'Thank you very much.' He absent-mindedly beamed at them but did not stay to see their astonished expressions.

'I wish for my usual teeth back please,' he gabbled as he hurried down the lane.

Glup! His mouth crumpled inwards. It was a wonderful feeling. His loose front tooth swung freely once again, then suddenly, squelch, it fell out. James spat it into his gravelly hand and smiled at it in amazement.

'Great.' He jumped once in the air, then ran on home down the lane.

As for the pterodactyl, it never did go back to its prehistoric age, but it does seem to have learnt now to keep out of sight, at least most of the time. It lives among the trees on the hill behind James's house, where the crows used to nest. (The crows nest somewhere else now, which is hardly surprising.) James visits it quite often.

So if you are ever in Somerset and you see, up in the sky, a very large bird which you can't quite identify, don't be too surprised.